Provinces and Territories of Canada

ONTARIO

— *"Yours to Discover"* —

Weigl Educational Publishers Limited
eet SE
berta

.weigl.com

Library and Archives Canada Cataloguing in Publication data available upon request.
Fax 403-233-7769 for the attention of the Publishing Records department.

ISBN 978-1-55388-975-5 (hard cover)
ISBN 978-1-55388-988-5 (soft cover)

Printed in the United States of America
1 2 3 4 5 6 7 8 9 0 13 12 11 10 09

Editor: Heather C. Hudak
Design: Terry Paulhus

All of the Internet URLs given in the book were valid at the time of publication. However, due to the dynamic nature of the Internet, some
addresses may have changed, or sites may have ceased to exist since publication. While the author and publisher regret any inconvenience this
may cause readers, no responsibility for any such changes can be accepted by either the author or the publisher.

Every reasonable effort has been made to trace ownership and to obtain permission to reprint copyright material. The publishers would be
pleased to have any errors or omissions brought to their attention so that they may be corrected in subsequent printings.

Weigl acknowledges Getty Images as its primary image supplier for this title.
Canada Post Corporation: page 30; Glenbow Museum: page 25 top; National Archives of Canada: page 26, 27 bottom, 28, 29,
31 top, 31 bottom; Southern Ontario Tourism Organization: page 37 bottom.

We gratefully acknowledge the financial support of the Government of Canada through the Book Publishing Industry Development
Program (BPIDP) for our publishing activities.

Contents

Ontario

There is a good reason for Ontario's nickname as the Heartland Province. In many ways, it is the heart of Canada. Ontario is the economic centre of the country, and it leads other provinces in agriculture and manufacturing. Ontario shares a border with Quebec to the east and Minnesota in the United States to the south. Waterways, including the Saint Lawrence River and the Great Lakes, also border Ontario to the south. To the west of Ontario lies Manitoba, and Hudson Bay and James Bay lie in the north. Ontario's bays and rivers give it important access to the Atlantic Ocean. They also make Ontario an important port province. Most Ontarians live in the Golden Horseshoe. This strip of land is shaped like a horseshoe and stretches from east of Toronto to Saint Catherines. It consists of the wealthiest and most industrialized areas in the province. Hamilton, the steel capital of Canada, is situated in the middle of the shoe. Other important cities in the south include Kitchener, London, Windsor, and Stratford.

Ontario covers 1,068,580 square kilometres. About 158,654 square kilometres of this area is fresh water.

Canada's Parliament Buildings are located in Ottawa, on top of Parliament Hill.

European explorers entered Ontario along its lakes and rivers. Their first route was up the Ottawa River, across Lake Nipissing, and down the French River into Georgian Bay and Lake Huron. Later, explorers canoed up the St. Lawrence River into Lake Ontario and Lake Erie. Explorers of the North began their journeys at James Bay and Hudson Bay ports.

In 1791, Ontario was created when the colony of Quebec was divided. When it was reunited with Quebec in 1840, it was known as Canada West. With **Confederation** in 1867, Ontario became its own, separate province. This decision produced four provinces that would be part of the Dominion of Canada—Nova Scotia, New Brunswick, Quebec, and Ontario. Ottawa was made the capital of the Dominion of Canada and, since then, has been regarded as the political hub of the country.

Lake Michigan is the only Great Lake that does not form part of Ontario's border. Toronto lies on the northwest shore of Lake Ontario.

Yonge Street runs 1,896 kilometres from Toronto to Rainy River. It is the longest street in the world.

Ontario is the most **urbanized** province in Canada. More than 80 percent of Ontarians live in urban centres. Toronto is the capital of Ontario. With its surrounding communities, it is the largest urban area in Ontario, and in all of Canada. More than five million people live in the city.

The nation's capital, Ottawa, lies to the northeast of Toronto on the Ontario–Quebec border. Other cities that lie farther to the north include Sault Sainte Marie, Timmins, and Thunder Bay.

Ontario is the southernmost province in all of Canada.

Together, the cities of Kitchener and Waterloo form one major community.

Ontario is the second-largest province in area in Canada. Only Quebec is larger.

Ontario's highest point is the Ishpatina Ridge, which is 693 metres above sea level.

Ontario's Manitoulin Island is the world's largest freshwater island. It is located in Lake Huron.

Toronto's Lester B. Pearson International Airport is Canada's busiest airport, with flights to the world's major centres. Other major airports are found in Ottawa, Windsor, Sudbury, and Thunder Bay.

The province's many waterways provide its residents with a place to have fun and relax, as well as a means of transportation.

Ontario has about 250,000 lakes.

Ontario is an Iroquois word meaning "beautiful" or "shining water."

LAND AND CLIMATE

There are three main regions in Ontario—the **Canadian Shield**, the Hudson Bay Lowlands, and the Great Lakes–Saint Lawrence Lowlands. The Canadian Shield covers most of the province. It contains thick forests, lakes, and bogs, so it is not ideal farmland. It is, however, rich with mineral deposits.

The Hudson Bay Lowlands is a region of rock and swampy land known as **muskeg**. The area slopes from the Canadian Shield to Hudson Bay. Together, the Canadian Shield and Hudson Bay Lowlands cover 90 percent of Ontario.

South of the Canadian Shield lie the Great Lakes–Saint Lawrence Lowlands. Most of Ontario's population live in this area. Its rolling land and fertile soil make it an ideal location for farming.

Ontario enjoys a distinct change of season because of its location in the interior of North America. The northern part of the province experiences short, warm summers, and long, cold winters. Toward the south, the temperatures and precipitation increase. The climate of the southwest is among the mildest in Canada.

The Great Lakes–Saint Lawrence Lowlands house the Niagara Escarpment. These limestone cliffs rise up to 532 metres. The escarpment spans 725 kilometres and is responsible for one of the country's most stunning sites—the Niagara Falls.

A large portion of the Saint Lawrence Lowlands has been cleared for cities and farms.

Autumn is a beautiful time of year in Ontario.

The highest temperature ever recorded in Ontario was 42.2° Celsius at Atikokan on July 11, 1936. The record low was −58.3° Celsius, recorded at Iroquois Falls on January 23, 1935.

NATURAL RESOURCES

The Hemlo Gold Mines have produced more than 1.7 billion grams of gold since opening in 1985.

Ontario has a wealth of natural resources. The Sudbury District produces about two-thirds of Canada's nickel, one-third of its copper, and most of its cobalt, a **by-product** of nickel-copper mining. It also mines lead, zinc, silver, and platinum. Mines at the Hemlo gold field near Marathon produce a quarter of Canada's gold.

KEEP CONNECTED

Ontario stone, granite, and marble were used in the construction of the legislative buildings in Toronto and Ottawa. Learn more about the construction of Parliament Hill in Ottawa at www.collineduparlement-parliamenthill.gc.ca/histoire-history/1859-1916-eng.html.

The glacial deposits of the south are a huge source of non-metallic construction minerals such as sand and gravel. The region also leads the country in the production of salt.

Natural gas and petroleum are mined in southern Ontario and beneath the waters of Lake Erie.

About three-quarters of Ontario is forested. The province uses half of this forested land to produce lumber. Forty communities are dependent on the lumber industry.

The fast-flowing rivers once produced power for Ontario's lumber mills. Today, they generate much of the electric power for the province. The waters are also a valuable resource for transportation and for commercial and sport fishing.

GET THE FACTS

Canada's first petroleum and gas fields were developed at Petrolia.

Sir Adam Beck Generation Station No. 2 generates a huge amount of hydroelectric power from the Niagara River.

Ontario has half of Canada's best farmland.

Sarnia's Chemical Valley has large petroleum refineries and produces chemicals, rubber, and synthetics.

PLANTS AND ANIMALS

Ottawa is known for the thousands of tulips that decorate the city each spring and summer. Every May, Ottawa holds the Canadian Tulip Festival.

The white trillium is the provincial flower. It is found in Ontario's deciduous forests and woodlands during the spring season.

Much of Ontario's landscape is covered with trees. Dense evergreen forests span across northern Ontario, except in the harsh climate of the far north. There, only a few spindly trees and bushes will grow. The shores of the Hudson Bay are characterized by **tundra**—poor soil over permanently frozen ground. Only low shrubs, wispy grasses, lichens, and mosses can survive there.

Central Ontario has a mixture of evergreens, such as cedar and fir, and **deciduous** trees, such as maple and oak. In the Canadian Shield, the forest consists of both deciduous and **coniferous** trees. These trees include spruce, walnut, pine, and tamarack. The south was once covered with deciduous woodland, maple, elm, beech, and oak, with pines on the lighter soils. Now, much of it has been cleared for farming.

Wildflowers decorate Ontario throughout most of the year. Trilliums and bloodroots bloom in the spring, while blossoms of aster and wild carrot cover many areas in the autumn. Lakeside hills in the north are full of wild blueberry bushes, and shrubs and mosses grow in the far northern areas of the province.

Ontario has more than 100 native species of fish. Among these fish are bass, walleye, trout, muskellunge, and pike. There are also many imported species, including the rainbow and brown trout and the chinook and coho salmon.

Animal life thrives in Ontario. Moose, black bears, deer, and wolves live throughout the north and can even be seen in the Great Lakes–Saint Lawrence Lowlands. White-tailed deer are common in the south. Skunks, porcupines, rabbits, muskrats, beavers, and foxes can be found in all regions of the province. Ducks and geese, raptors, such as hawks and owls, and even turkey vultures are a common sight in parts of Ontario.

There are more than 20 species of frogs and salamanders in Ontario.

KEEP CONNECTED

Learn more about the types of frogs found throughout Ontario and other parts of Canada by visiting www.naturewatch.ca/english/frogwatch/on.

Polar bears can be seen in Ontario on the shores of James Bay.

The common loon is the provincial bird. It can be seen swimming on many Ontario lakes and rivers.

Southern Ontario faces many environmental challenges. When precipitation falls through **emissions** from factories and motor vehicles, it becomes acidic. The acid rain is not good for plants or animals. Also, fertilizers, street salt, washing detergents, factory run-off, and untreated waste find their way into the rivers and lakes. Canada and Ontario have signed an agreement to restore problem areas, prevent pollution, and protect human health and the environment on the Great Lakes.

Many organizations and individuals are concerned with maintaining the health of Ontario's wildlife and the Great Lakes.

The permanently frozen ground of the tundra is called permafrost.

Snowshoe hares live throughout the province.

The north shore of Lake Erie has more plant life than any other region in Canada.

Ontario's extreme southwest is home to some of the rarest trees in Canada. These include sassafrass, tulip trees, sycamore, and cucumber trees.

There are at least 25 species of reptiles in the province.

The forests of Ontario provide people with recreation areas and animals with habitat.

The white pine is the provincial tree. It has been a valuable natural resource throughout Ontario's history.

TOURISM

Ontario has many spectacular sites to visit. About 12 million people visit Niagara Falls each year. In 1846, the very first tourist boat—*The Maid of the Mist*—took people to the base of the falls. Now, helicopter tours buzz above the breathtaking view.

The Thousand Islands is a region of rocky islands that draws tourists who wish to relax and enjoy the beauty of the Saint Lawrence River. The islands vary in size from tiny to quite large. Almost all of the islands have holiday cottages.

Toronto's CN Tower is one of the world's highest structures. It stands 553 metres high. Brave visitors can stand on the glass floor of the Outdoor Observation Deck and look 342 metres down to the ground.

In Ottawa, Canada's Parliament Buildings attract many visitors during the year. With their tall copper roofs and Gothic structure, these buildings are an impressive site and a symbol of national pride. In the summer months, visitors can watch the Changing of the Guard ceremony, which is held daily on Parliament Hill.

Young visitors love the interactive exhibits in such areas as space, meteorology, and automotives at Toronto's Ontario Science Centre, Sudbury's Science North, and Ottawa's Canada Museum of Science and Technology.

Canada's Wonderland is a huge amusement park north of Toronto. It has a waterpark, live shows, and more than 65 rides.

The world's longest freshwater beach is at Wasaga Beach on Georgian Bay. It is a favourite with people who love water sports.

The Changing of the Guard ceremony involves a parade of 125 guards in red jackets who replace the guards already on duty.

INDUSTRY

KEEP CONNECTED
Food and beverage processing is the province's second-largest industry. Learn about the food and beverage industry in Ontario at **www.aofp.ca**.

Ontario is the country's leading manufacturing province. It has easily available power, a large, skilled work force, and an excellent transportation network.

The province's main manufacturing industry is the automobile and auto parts industry. Much of the raw material used comes from steel industries in Hamilton and Sault Sainte Marie. The steel is also used in other industries, including the machinery, farm implement, metal fabrication, and aircraft industries.

Ontario has the most farmland of all the provinces, but its farms are among Canada's smallest.

Southern Ontario's farms produce much of the food needed by its large population centres. There are dairy and livestock operations throughout the region, as well as farms that produce corn, mixed grain, and **forage** crops for feed. The Niagara Peninsula climate is perfect for growing fruits and vegetables.

Ontario produces about 50 percent of Canada's goods and 80 percent of its manufactured exports.

Most of the minerals harvested in the north are **refined** in Sudbury and Port Colborne.

Ontario's aerospace industry is the sixth largest in the world.

Water transport is still very important in Ontario. Hudson Bay, the Great Lakes-St. Lawrence Seaway, and the Trent and Rideau Canal systems give most parts of the province access to the sea.

Thunder Bay on Lake Superior handles the greatest tonnage of cargo on the lakes.

Fishing was once an important industry in Ontario, but it has been hit both by overfishing and by pollution, especially in Lake Erie.

The Ottawa region has become known as Silicon Valley North. Computers, communications technology, and software are all produced there.

GOODS AND SERVICES

About 21,000 kilometres of highways, and more than 160,000 kilometres of other roadways run through Ontario.

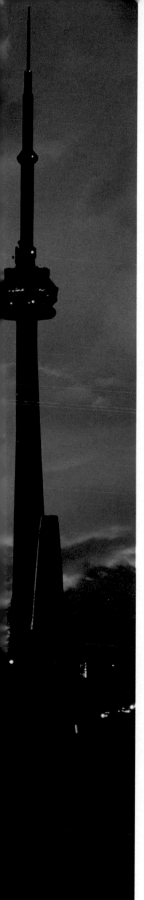

Grain accounts for about 70 percent of the cargo shipped by lakers.

Goods are only valuable if they are available for people to buy. Ontario's goods are transported in a number of ways. Huge ships, called lakers, sail on the Great Lakes–Saint Lawrence Seaway system. They carry bulk cargoes such as coal, wheat, and canola from Thunder Bay, and steel from Hamilton.

Railways also carry Ontario's resources to other regions. Since most of the manufacturing and markets are in southern Ontario or the United States, transporters also take advantage of Ontario's excellent highways by shipping goods by truck.

Ontario has rivers that are ideal for generating electricity. Hydroelectric dams make use of the enormous power of the Niagara River. The province also uses nuclear and coal-fired generators for electricity production.

Ontario has 20 universities and 24 colleges of arts and applied technology, two of which are French.

Toronto is Canada's financial capital. Many large corporations and insurance companies, as well as Canada's major banks, have their head offices in Toronto. The Toronto Stock Exchange is a fast-paced and exciting environment. It is the largest stock exchange in the country.

Toronto's Bay Street area is the financial centre of Canada.

The Toronto Eaton's Centre is one of the country's leading shopping malls. It also serves as a tourist attraction that draws about one million visitors every week.

Ottawa is home to many important national institutions. The National Library of Canada is located there. This library is dedicated to preserving Canadian documents. It houses books, periodicals, recordings, and other materials related to Canadian heritage. Its collections are available to everyone in the country. The National Archives also preserve millions of documents, maps, and photographs associated with Canada. Other national institutions in Ottawa include the Canadian Institute for Scientific and Technical Information, the Supreme Court of Canada, and the National Research Council.

GET THE FACTS

Ontarians spend about $1.2 billion per year in food stores. They spend twice as much on vehicles and vehicle parts.

About 90 percent of Ontario's exports go to the United States.

Southern Ontario has more kilometres of roads in proportion to its area than any other part of Canada.

Twelve daily newspapers serve the Toronto area. Other cities have one daily paper each, and most communities have weeklies.

Travelling on the Polar Bear Express from Cochrane to Moosonee, passengers can experience the northern Ontario wilderness from the comfort of a passenger rail car.

A stretch of Highway 401 through north Toronto carries about 380,000 vehicles a day. This makes it one of the busiest highways in North America.

Health services for Ontarians are financed by the province, with some assistance from the federal government.

FIRST NATIONS

Before any Europeans arrived, the Ontario region was inhabited by a number of Aboriginal groups. Aboriginal Peoples in the Ontario area were joined by a common language and culture. Algonquian-speaking peoples lived in the north. Iroquoian speakers lived in the south.

The northern Aboriginal Peoples were mostly hunters and gatherers who moved from place to place in search of food. The Ojibwa lived near Lake Superior. The Cree lived around James Bay and the prairies. The Algonquin in the Ottawa Valley were important fur trading partners of the French. Manitoulin Island was home for the Ottawa.

The southern Aboriginal Peoples moved less often. They lived by growing corn, beans, and squash. They also hunted and fished. The Huron Confederacy, who traded as far away as Quebec, lived to the east of Georgian Bay. The Iroquois, traditional enemies of the Huron, lived in northern New York State.

Other Aboriginal Peoples in the Ontario region included the Petun, who lived in southwest, and the Neutrals, who lived along Lake Ontario and beside the Niagara River.

Aboriginal Peoples called corn, squash, and beans the "Three Sisters."

The Iroquois lived in family groups in large longhouses.

When the Huron befriended French fur traders, the Iroquois **allied** with the British. They both became part of the European fight for the fur trade. As well as setting up a fur-trading network, Samuel de Champlain, a French explorer, helped the Huron fight against the Iroquois. These attacks failed and, in 1648, the Iroquois **retaliated**. The Iroquois were fierce fighters and better armed than the Huron. They used guns they had bought from Dutch traders, killing many Huron.

The Ojibwa collected the sap of maple trees. They made maple syrup to sweeten their foods.

Champlain partnered with the Huron in their battle against the Iroquois.

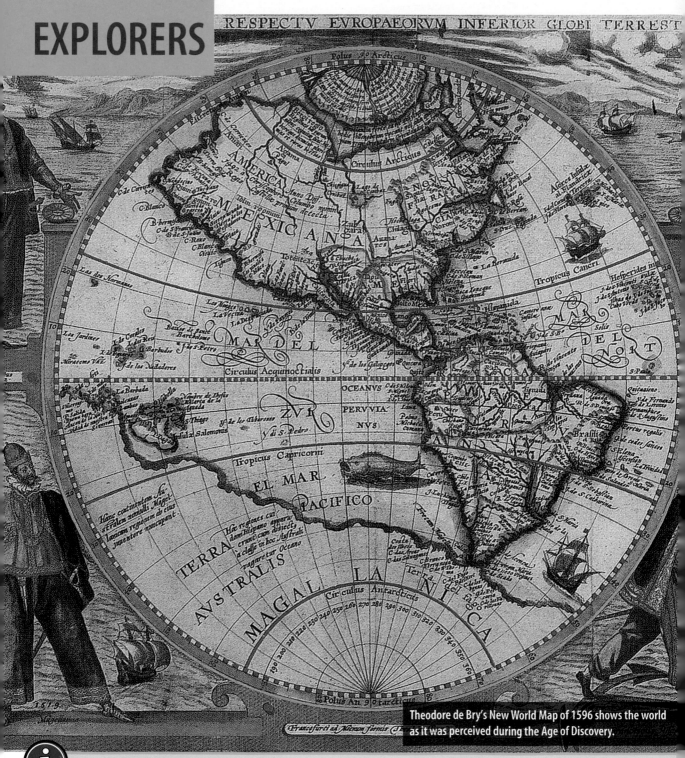

RESPECTV EVROPAEORVM INFERIOR GLOBI TERREST

Theodore de Bry's New World Map of 1596 shows the world as it was perceived during the Age of Discovery.

KEEP CONNECTED

Explorer Jean Nicolet was so sure that he would find the Orient that he came ashore on Ontario dressed in a magnificent, silk Chinese robe. Find out more about Nicolet, other explorers, and the history of Ontario at **www.archives.gov.on.ca/english/on-line-exhibits/franco-ontarian/index.aspx.**

Henry Hudson landed on Hudson Bay in 1610. He was the first European in present-day Ontario, but he did not explore the area. He was looking for the Northwest Passage, a western route to the Orient. Hudson disappeared when his crew turned against him and cast him adrift on the northern sea.

Samuel de Champlain's first contact with the Huron Confederacy was in Quebec. In 1610, he sent a member of the expedition, Étienne Brulé, to live among the Huron. Brulé learned their language and translated for Champlain. The Hurons' large, **pallisaded** towns and cultivated fields amazed Champlain. He made notes and maps of everything he saw.

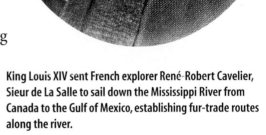

René-Robert Cavelier, Sieur de la Salle, was also looking for a passage to the Orient. He followed the Saint Lawrence River to Fort Frontenac and set out along Lake Ontario. On the river above Niagara Falls, he built the *Griffon*, the first ship to sail the upper lakes. He travelled through Lakes Erie and Huron to what is now Mackinac Island and into Lake Michigan.

King Louis XIV sent French explorer René-Robert Cavelier, Sieur de La Salle to sail down the Mississippi River from Canada to the Gulf of Mexico, establishing fur-trade routes along the river.

Missionaries began to arrive in the early 1600s. Ontario's first missionary, Joseph Le Caron, arrived in Huronia in 1615. The Jesuits built a fortified mission at Sainte-Marie Among the Hurons, near present-day Midland, and sent preachers out into the region. Sainte-Marie Among the Hurons was the centre of the Jesuit missions to the Huron peoples.

When diseases started to kill the Hurons, many feared that the missionaries' rituals were witchcraft and blamed them for the deaths. Five Jesuit fathers were killed by the Iroquois.

Britain gained the upper hand over France when it captured Quebec City in the battle of the Plains of Abraham.

The British and French fought the Seven Years' War for control of North America. The British won the war in 1763.

The British and French fought each other for control of Ontario. During these battles, settlement in the area was very slow, except for the establishment of trading posts.

In 1763, after many long years of battle and dispute, the British claimed victory over France. The lands of New France now belonged to the British Empire. At that time, there were only a few French settlements scattered around the southern regions.

It was not until the American Revolution that significant settlement began to take place in Ontario. The American Revolution was fought between the United States and Britain. Many people in the United States wanted to be free from British control, and from 1776 to 1783, they fought for their freedom. However, many Americans wanted to remain British subjects. Their strong loyalty to the British Crown led them to move to Canada. By 1785, between 6,000 and 10,000 **Loyalists** had arrived in Ontario.

POPULATION

Two-thirds of the people in Toronto were not born in the city.

As people settled in Ontario, they built their communities on waterways. This water provided their power, irrigation, and transportation. As railway lines were developed, people moved closer to them to make it easier to transport their goods to markets.

Since the mid-nineteenth century, the province's population has been giving up the country life. Today, more than 80 percent of Ontario's population live in urban areas. As well, the population of the province continues to rise. Adding to natural growth is immigration. Most immigrants to Canada decide to make Ontario their new home.

Of all the cities in the province, Toronto has the most people. They represent about 40 percent of Ontario's population, and about 15 percent of Canada's population.

Half of the northern population live in the area's five major cities—Thunder Bay, Sault Sainte Marie, Sudbury, Timmins, and North Bay.

GET THE FACTS

People from all over the world have come to live in Toronto.

With about 12.1 million people, Ontario is Canada's most heavily populated province.

About 90 percent of Ontarians live in the southern part of the province.

More than half of Ontario's population live in the Golden Horseshoe.

Ontario has more than 571 municipalities, which include cities, villages, towns, and townships.

POLITICS AND GOVERNMENT

In 1998, the seven municipal governments of Metropolitan Toronto were made into one, the City of Toronto.

Ontario's Legislative Building is located in Toronto. Here, members of the provincial Parliament debate and make laws that affect all Ontarians.

Ontario has an elected, one-chamber parliament, with 107 members. These members represent different political parties. The premier is the leader of the majority party. He or she appoints a cabinet, or executive council, of 24 ministers. With the exception of one Liberal and one New Democratic Party government, the Conservatives have been in power since 1943. Ontario also has 24 appointed senate seats and elects 103 federal members of Parliament.

Ontario has 27 counties and several levels of local government. The local governments have the power to tax property and provide local services, such as water, waste management, and local roads, to their citizens. Most cities and towns in Ontario have their own police forces.

GET THE FACTS

Six Canadian prime ministers, Arthur Meighen, William Lyon Mackenzie King, Lester B. Pearson, John Diefenbaker, Paul Martin, and Stephen Harper were born in Ontario.

Ontario's motto is *Ut incepit fidelis sic permanet*. This means "Loyal it began, loyal it remains."

The provincial government's belief in lower taxes and less government has led to a reduction in the number of school boards and municipalities in Ontario.

CULTURAL GROUPS

Eighty percent of Ontarians claim English as their first language. Most of the 4.6 percent who speak French live near the Quebec border or in the North. Ontario has the largest French-speaking community in Canada outside Quebec. A visitor to Hearst or Longlac in northern Ontario would hardly hear a word of English. French is the main language of both communities. The sound of many other languages can be heard throughout the province.

At one time, Ontario had a strong British population, but that is changing. In 2008, for example, nearly 265,000 immigrants came to Canada from all over the world. Many of them made homes in Toronto neighbourhoods, where people of their own culture were already living.

Other cities, such as Thunder Bay, have strong Ukrainian, Italian, Finnish, Polish, and Dutch populations. These groups have formed their own ethnic communities. Saint Jacobs, near Kitchener-Waterloo, has a prosperous Mennonite community and a busy farmers' market.

Ontario has about 132 Aboriginal nations. Their heritage is displayed at interpretive centres, such as Petroglyphs Provincial Park and the Woodlands Cultural Centre.

Ontario has many festivals that celebrate the cultural diversity of its people. An important cultural celebration is the Canadian Aboriginal Festival. This festival features 1,000 dancers, drummers, and singers. It also features the Canadian Aboriginal Music Awards and Aboriginal art, food, and crafts. Caribana attracts huge crowds to watch 4,000 people of Caribbean descent dressed in colourful costumes sing and dance their way through downtown Toronto.

Toronto's Greek community is the largest in North America. Every year, this community hosts the Greektown Taste of the Danforth. Visitors can taste delicious foods like gyros, souvlaki, pastitsio, and spanikopita. The Greek Cultural Summer Festival in Ottawa also showcases traditional food, as well as dances, entertainment, and art.

Caribana is one of North America's largest cultural events. More than one million people attend the festival every year.

Oktoberfest in Kitchener-Waterloo welcomes thousands of visitors each year. It is the largest annual Bavarian Festival in North America. Only Oktoberfest in Munich, Germany, is bigger.

Toronto is home to five Chinatowns.

There are about 60 different languages and cultures represented in Ontario.

Chatham-Kent's Festival of Nations and Windsor's Carousel of Nations are among Ontario's many celebrations of diversity.

The Great Rendez-Vous Festival at Fort William Historical Park, near Thunder Bay, re-enacts the days when voyageurs rested in the area before they began the long paddle back to Quebec.

In the early 1800s, Mennonites from Pennsylvania established a settlement in what is now Kitchener-Waterloo. Today, this Mennonite community is very active, and its farmers' market is well-visited.

The Six Nations Annual Fall Fair features outdoor performances based on Aboriginal history and tradition.

ARTS AND ENTERTAINMENT

There is no shortage of music in Ontario. Toronto, Ottawa, Hamilton, and Kitchener-Waterloo all have symphony orchestras. Toronto is also the headquarters of the National Ballet of Canada and the Canadian Opera Company.

Ontario has given the music world some of its biggest stars. Among them are Avril Lavigne, Alanis Morissette, Amanda Marshall, and the pop group, the Barenaked Ladies. Neil Young and Bryan Adams were born in the province but made their names elsewhere. Country singers Shania Twain and Michelle Wright have received many international awards, and folk singer Gordon Lightfoot has many devoted fans throughout the country.

Mike Myers, the world-famous comedian, was born in Scarborough.

So many major films and television series are made in Toronto that it is called Hollywood North. Every September, filmmakers from around the world showcase their work at the famous Toronto International Film Festival. Some of Hollywood's leading stars, including Jim Carrey, Mike Myers, and Neve Campbell, come from Ontario. Keanu Reeves and Matthew Perry also grew up in the province. Dan Aykroyd and the late John Candy both got their start with Toronto's Second City comedy troupe.

Toronto has an excellent theatre scene. It produces many popular musical shows. The Shaw Festival in Niagara-on-the-Lake and the Stratford Shakespeare Festival, each with three theatres, draw audiences from across Canada and the United States. Some of the world's most respected Shakespearean actors take part in the Stratford Shakespeare Festival. The Shaw Festival is the only festival in the world that specializes in the production of plays written by George Bernard Shaw.

Graham Greene, one of the stars of *Dances with Wolves*, is from the Six Nations Reserve on the Grand River.

Shania Twain is from Timmins. The town is so proud of its star that it has renamed its main street "Shania Twain Way."

Some of the best-known artists from Ontario are perhaps Harold Town, Homer Watson, and many members of the **Group of Seven**. Many of the landscape paintings by the group are displayed at the McMichael Canadian Art Collection in Kleinburg and Ottawa's National Gallery of Canada. Exhibitions of major international works of art can often be seen at the National Gallery and the Art Gallery of Ontario in Toronto.

Farley Mowat, Margaret Atwood, and Morley Callaghan are all widely read Ontario authors. They have all written bestselling books.

Pauline Johnson was the daughter of a Six Nations' chief and an English mother. She read her poetry across Canada and overseas, dressed as a Aboriginal princess.

Alex Trebek, the quizmaster of *Jeopardy*, and Morley Safer, of the news show *60 Minutes*, both come from Ontario.

Canada's largest museum, the Royal Ontario Museum, and the Children's Own Museum next door, are bursting with things for young people to explore.

SPORTS

Algonquin Park is a great place for camping, hiking, and birdwatching. About 240 bird species have been seen within the park.

Ontario's ski season has been made longer by computer controlled snow-making machines. They can put many centimetres of snow on a slope overnight.

Nature has given Ontario an ideal geography for outdoor sports and recreation. The province has 250,000 lakes for boating, fishing, and swimming. Beautiful beaches line the southern lake shores. Algonquin Park, Ontario's oldest provincial park, has 1,500 kilometres of canoe routes and excellent fishing and camping. Nature lovers can even join park naturalists in nighttime wolf howling.

Tennis and golf are popular summer sports in Ontario. Junior golf leagues, sponsored by major companies, are encouraging the next generation of professional and recreational players.

The steep slopes of the Niagara Escarpment in the snowbelt draw thousands of winter sports enthusiasts. World downhill skiing champions Steve Podborski and Todd Brooker and Olympic champions Nancy Greene Raine and Kathy Kreiner have all skied on Ontario's slopes.

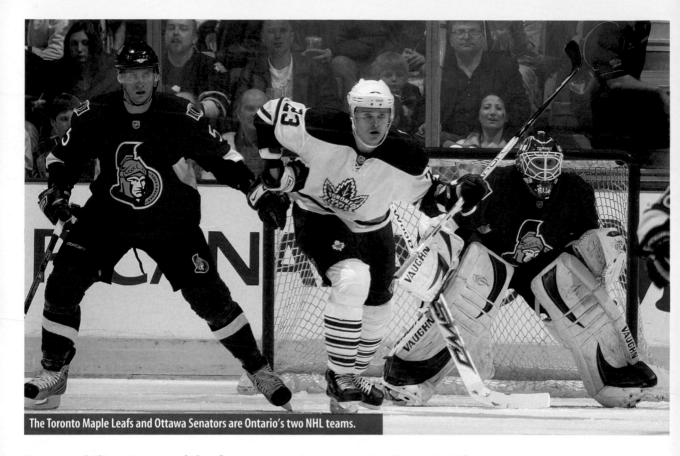

The Toronto Maple Leafs and Ottawa Senators are Ontario's two NHL teams.

Snowmobiling is one of the fastest-growing sports in Ontario. There are about 50,000 kilometres of trails and about 150,000 snowmobiles in the province.

The National Hockey League (NHL) has two teams in Ontario—the Toronto Maple Leafs and the Ottawa Senators. After many years at Maple Leaf Gardens, the Leafs moved into Air Canada Centre, which they share with the Toronto Raptors of the National Basketball Association. The Ottawa Senators play in a modern, custom-built facility called Scotiabank Place.

Other professional sports are played in Toronto's Rogers Centre. The Rogers Centre is the first stadium to have a fully **retractable** roof. It is also home to the Toronto Blue Jays, the city's Major League Baseball team, and the Toronto Argonauts of the Canadian Football League (CFL). Ontario's other CFL team is the Hamilton Tiger Cats.

KEEP CONNECTED

Find out more about the Toronto Maples leafs, the Ottawa Senators, and other professional hockey teams by visiting **www.nhl.com**.

For four consecutive years, Toronto's Rogers Centre received the Stadium of the Year Award.

In the first year at its new home, 500,000 visitors toured Toronto's Hockey Hall of Fame. Hockey fans from all over the world can see the memorabilia, test the strength of their slap shot, and play in goal to simulated shots from Wayne Gretzky and Mark Messier. The Hall of Fame displays hockey jerseys, goalie masks, and photos of hockey heroes.

GET THE FACTS

The Hockey Hall of Fame was founded in 1943 and was the result of meetings of the NHL and the Canadian Amateur Hockey Association.

The Canadian Football Hall of Fame is located in Hamilton.

The first person to go over Niagara Falls in a barrel and survive was Annie Taylor, in 1901.

The NHL's all-time leading goal scorer, Wayne Gretzky, was born in Brantford, Ontario.

There are more than 200 Ontario athletes in the Canadian Sports Hall of Fame.

Indy car racing draws thousands of spectators to Toronto's lakeshore track. Paul Tracy of Scarborough, Ontario, is one of the sport's star drivers.

Ontario has produced top athletes in many sports. Brian Orser and Elvis Stojko were both world figure skating champions. Al Hackner and Marylin Bodogh were two-time world curling champions.

The Toronto International Boat Show is one of the biggest in North America.

CANADA

Canada is a vast nation, and each province and territory has its own unique features. This map shows important information about each of Canada's 10 provinces and three territories, including when they joined Confederation, their size, population, and capital city. For more information about Canada, visit **http://canada.gc.ca**.

Alberta
Entered Confederation: 1905
Capital: Edmonton
Area: 661,848 sq km
Population: 3,632,483

British Columbia
Entered Confederation: 1871
Capital: Victoria
Area: 944,735 sq km
Population: 4,419,974

Manitoba
Entered Confederation: 1870
Capital: Winnipeg
Area: 647,797 sq km
Population: 1,213,815

New Brunswick
Entered Confederation: 1867
Capital: Fredericton
Area: 72,908 sq km
Population: 748,319

Newfoundland and Labrador
Entered Confederation: 1949
Capital: St. John's
Area: 405,212 sq km
Population: 508,990

SYMBOLS OF ONTARIO

FLAG COAT OF ARMS FLOWER
White Trillium

Northwest Territories
Entered Confederation: 1870
Capital: Yellowknife
Area: 1,346,106 sq km
Population: 42,940

Nova Scotia
Entered Confederation: 1867
Capital: Halifax
Area: 55,284 sq km
Population: 939,531

Nunavut
Entered Confederation: 1999
Capital: Iqaluit
Area: 2,093,190 sq km
Population: 531,556

Ontario
Entered Confederation: 1867
Capital: Toronto
Area: 1,076,395 sq km
Population: 12,986,857

Prince Edward Island
Entered Confederation: 1873
Capital: Charlottetown
Area: 5,660 sq km
Population: 140,402

Quebec
Entered Confederation: 1867
Capital: Quebec City
Area: 1,542,056 sq km
Population: 7,782,561

Saskatchewan
Entered Confederation: 1905
Capital: Regina
Area: 651,036 sq km
Population: 1,023,810

Yukon
Entered Confederation: 1898
Capital: Whitehorse
Area: 482,443 sq km
Population: 33,442

Alert
esmere
sland

0   200   400 Kilometers
0   200   400 Miles

Baffin Bay

Baffin
Island

Davis Strait

Iqaluit
(Frobisher Bay)

Ivujivik

Labrador
Sea

dson
Bay

NEWFOUNDLAND

Schefferville
Happy Valley-
Goose Bay

Island of
Newfoundland

Chisasibi
(Fort George)

Gander
Saint John's

QUEBEC   Sept-Iles

Gulf of

Moosonee

St. Lawrence
PRINCE
EDWARD
ISLAND

St. Pierre and
Miquelon (FRANCE)

Chibougamau

Sydney

NEW
BRUNSWICK

Charlottetown

Quebec   Fredericton

Sherbrooke
Sudbury   Montreal

Saint
John

Halifax
NOVA
SCOTIA

Ottawa

Lake
Huron

Lake
Ontario

Toronto
Hamilton
London

Lake Erie

BIRD
Common Loon

TREE
Eastern White Pine

GEM
Amethyst

BRAIN TEASERS

Test your knowledge of Ontario by trying to answer these mind-boggling brain teasers!

1 Multiple Choice

What is the capital of Ontario?
a) Windsor
b) Toronto
c) Hamilton
d) Thunder Bay

2 True or False?

The Ottawa Senators are Ontario's only NHL team.

3 Multiple Choice

Ontario is the least urbanized province in Canada.

4 Multiple Choice

What is the name of the longest street in the world, which happens to run 1,896 kilometres from Toronto to Rainy River?
a) Olde Street
b) Spencer Street
c) Yonge Street
d) Finmark Street

5 Multiple Choice

What is Ontario best known for manufacturing?
a) automobiles
b) appliances
c) planes
d) furniture

6 True or False?

The nation's capital, Ottawa, is located in Ontario.

7 Multiple Choice

What percentage of Ontario's exports go to the United States?
a) 50
b) 20
c) 5
d) 90

8 Multiple Choice

Due to its large production of films and television series, Toronto is often referred to as

_____.
a) Little Hollywood
b) Hollywood North
c) The Second Hollywood
d) Hollywood East

1. B, The capital of Ontario is Toronto. 2. False, the Ottawa Senators and the Toronto Maple Leafs both are located in Ontario. 3. False, Ontario is the most urbanized province in Canada. 4. C, Yonge Street is the name of the longest street in the world. 5. A, Ontario is best known for manufacturing automobiles. 6. True 7. D, 90 percent of Ontario's exports go to the United States. 8. B, Due to its large production of films and television series, Toronto is often referred to as Hollywood North.

MORE INFORMATION

GLOSSARY

allied: united or connected by mutual agreement

by-product: something produced during the manufacturing of something else

Canadian Shield: a region of ancient rock that encircles the Hudson Bay and covers part of mainland Canada

Confederation: the joining together of Ontario, Quebec, Nova Scotia, and New Brunswick to make Canada

coniferous: evergreen trees with needles and cones

deciduous: trees or shrubs that shed leaves every year

emissions: particles that are sent out into the atmosphere

forage: food for horses or cattle

Group of Seven: a group of Canadian painters, most famous for their paintings of Canadian landscape throughout the 1920s

Loyalists: colonists who remained loyal to Great Britain during the American Revolution

muskeg: a swamp or a marsh

pallisaded: having a high, wooden protective fence

refined: made pure

retaliated: struck back when provoked

retractable: able to draw back or take in

tundra: an Arctic or subarctic plain with a permanently frozen subsoil

urbanized: living in cities or towns

BOOKS

Beckett, Harry. *Canada's Land and People: Ontario*. Calgary: Weigl Educational Publishers Limited, 2008.

Craats, Rennay. *Canadian Sites and Symbols: Ontario*. Calgary: Weigl Educational Publishers Limited, 2004.

Schwartzenberger, Tina. *Canadian Geographic Regions: The Canadian Shield*. Calgary: Weigl Educational Publishers Limited, 2006.

Tomljanovic, Tatiana. *Linking Canadian Communities: Manufacturing*. Calgary: Weigl Educational Publishers Limited, 2008.

WEBSITES

Government of Ontario
www.gov.on.ca

City of Toronto
www.city.toronto.on.ca

Royal Ontario Museum
www.rom.on.ca

Some websites stay current longer than others. To find more Ontario websites, use your Internet search engine to look up such topics as "Ontario," "Ottawa," "Rogers Centre," "Parliament Buildings," or any other topic you want to research.

INDEX